PALM
BEACH

"To my grandparents Estée and Joseph, who first introduced me to the magic of Palm Beach. They taught me the importance of family, passion, hard work, loving life, and following your dreams."

AERIN LAUDER

PALM BEACH

ASSOULINE

> **"Tennis, swimming, lunch. Golf, drinks, dinner. The Patio. Bradley's. Bed. Tennis, swimming, lunch. Golf, drinks, dinner. The movies. The Colony. Bradley's. Bed. Tennis, swimming, lunch. Fishing, drinks, dinner. Etcetera."**

Cecil Beaton

This was how Cecil Beaton described his time spent in Palm Beach in a 1937 issue of *Vogue*. And while the faces and places may have changed since then, the warmth, spirit, and character of Palm Beach remains true to its roots. When we stepped off of the plane, my grandparents were always the first people we would see as we arrived in Palm Beach. They would be waiting for my family at the gate; my grandmother Estée in white pants, a Pucci top, and a broad-brimmed straw hat, and my grandfather Joseph in a button-down shirt, navy blazer, and tortoise-shell Ray Bans. My sister, Jane, and I would immediately run into their arms. This was the moment our Palm Beach vacation began.

They would drive us back to their house and go straight to the kitchen where Estée—we never called her Grandma, always Estée—would pour us each a glass of fresh orange juice in her beautiful blue glassware.

Aerin Lauder at her house in Palm Beach.
Following pages: George Clarke sipping champagne at a local party, 1955.

Those early vacations to Palm Beach were always my favorite trips and remain among my most-treasured memories of my childhood. Whether we were at the pool or the beach, sitting in my grandparents' sunroom, or roaming along the bike path, we were together as a family, enjoying the sun and the beauty that was absolutely everywhere. Palm Beach is where Estée and I had our very best conversations. It's where our family spent time sitting together in the garden and enjoyed large communal meals—simply taking pleasure in one another's presence. One of my most cherished photographs from when I was a little girl was taken in front of Nandos, a restaurant we would always dine at that served delicious Italian food, had a piano player, and that I wish still existed.

I was always very close to Estée and am still inspired by her to this day. The joy that she got from life and family was infectious, and never more so than when we were all in Palm Beach. She instilled in me a love of Palm Beach that I've carried with me throughout my life and still harbor. For me, Palm Beach has always been a place of rich memories, idyllic times, and endless inspiration.

Palm Beach's earliest history goes back to 1879, when the *Providencia,* a Spanish ship en route from Havana, Cuba, to Cádiz, Spain, and carrying a load of Caribbean coconuts, wrecked off the Florida coast. Early settlers recognized an opportunity for a new industry and quickly naturalized the coconuts, planting them throughout the island and inadvertently defining its landscape forever. Today, Palm Beach has some of the tallest coconut palms in the United States.

Soon, the island began to develop rapidly—Henry Morrison Flagler, an industrialist and cofounder of Standard Oil, had taken an interest in Florida's Atlantic Coast and began buying up large plots of land in the area. By the

A Lilly Pulitzer map of Palm Beach.
Following pages: The veranda at Aerin's Palm Beach home.

early 1890s, a local community had begun to establish itself with the advent of several hotels, businesses, and winter residents. Flagler's mission to build a resort destination was realized with the opening of his Royal Poinciana Hotel, but what really cemented his success was the unveiling of the crucial Florida East Coast Railroad. The town was officially incorporated in 1911.

There's a great respect for the past in Palm Beach—an embracing of the Old World—but there's also a younger generation that keeps this special place modern and relevant. It is at once old and new, and years after I first came here for holidays with my family, my ideal day in Palm Beach is very similar to the days I spent with Estée.

When I was growing up, a favorite Palm Beach diversion was a visit to The Breakers Hotel. To go there today is still a treat. A sprawling, iconic landmark, The Breakers (initially founded as the Palm Beach Inn) is at the top of many must-see-in-Palm Beach lists, including my own. Built in 1896 as one of Henry Flagler's landmark developments, it sits on a breathtaking stretch of beach and was modeled after an Italian Renaissance palace—an architectural style seen again and again on the island. After a recent renovation, the updated guest rooms are more contemporary and coastal cool than in the past, but the place as a whole still exudes a wonderful old-world charm and was listed on the National Register of Historic Places in 1973. The Breakers is a prime destination for everything from tennis and golf to lounging by the pool in one of the hotel cabanas; and the spa and gym are perfection, too. I'm a loyal fan of the breakfast buffet served in the grand ballroom, but I also love the Beach Club for more casual fare. Surrounded by beautiful ocean views, it serves up the best conch fritters.

An ultimate resort town, Palm Beach has no shortage of places to overnight. For a more intimate stay, The Brazilian Court is a historic landmark featuring a lush, serene courtyard and apartment-style suites teeming with 1920s glamour. Designed by the Italian-born and up-and-coming Rosario Candela, the building elicits a very Mediterranean aesthetic and holds classical details throughout. The Colony Hotel, whose interior was renovated by local designer Celerie Kemble and which sits as a vividly colorful box directly adjacent to Worth Avenue, intimates a whimsically classic feeling that comes complete with a traditional high tea served on the porch. Since the hotel's founding, it has played host to the likes of Frank Sinatra, John Lennon, and Judy Garland, and has been a home-away-from-home for British royalty.

Many of the island hotels have bikes on hand for their guests to fully explore Palm Beach. Should you find yourself at one, I can't recommend highly enough a ride—or even just a walk—on the Lake Trail. A must, this peaceful and scenic trail hails back to the nineteenth century, when it was the first road on the island. Today, it is perfectly landscaped and follows the edge of Lake Worth. On one side, water and boats and the Intracoastal Waterway; on the other, glimpses of historic Palm Beach homes behind stately hedges. Palm Beach can feel like a small town in many ways, and the Lake Trail exemplifies that for me. I'm so often delighted by how many people I run into during my daily walk.

Of the many elements of Palm Beach that have remained the same since my childhood, the ever-present bougainvillea, the sculpture gardens, and the very specific Mediterranean style of architecture are all wonderfully unchanged. With its rich blend of Venetian, Spanish, and Moorish influences, Palm Beach is about color—I believe one of its most defining and endearing qualities is a bold and

Following pages (left): Estée Lauder standing before her dining room table in Palm Beach, c. 1970s. *(clockwise from top left):* The Lauder family, 1972; Estée and Joseph Lauder holding a young Aerin in Palm Beach, c. 1970s; The Lauders attending a Palm Beach ball.

playful palette. You can walk the streets and see brightly painted façades and beautiful flowers—even the fruit being served is stunningly bright. There is a spirited vibrancy of color that is quite literally built into the city. Additionally, everywhere you turn seems to hold a new beautiful, intricate tile-scape just waiting to be discovered. I am very tile obsessed, and a walk around Palm Beach is a great visual indulgence. Intricate tilework is one of the hallmarks of the island's style—it reaches out and influences everything. Women are in bright colors twelve months of the year—long dresses in turquoise or coral, gold sandals, straw bags day or night. There are so many different versions of Palm Beach fashion, so many eras to draw from, and so much style everywhere. Part of the fun of keeping your eyes open around the island is seeing what people draw from and who becomes inspired by what.

In her book *Palm Beach Chic,* Jennifer Ash said, "It's [the] eclectic mix of old and new, of Spanish and Caribbean, of contemporary design and sun-faded WASP thrift, that makes Palm Beach chic." Such a fusion of styles can be spotted in many Palm Beach homes, at once inspiring and awe-inducing. I find myself just as enamored of the beautiful apartments on Via Mizner that were built by Addison Mizner in the 1920s as I am by the grand and sweeping estates. Among my favorite of the latter is La Follia, the famous estate built by Broadway producer Terry Allen Kramer. Its porch is one of my favorite porches in the world: stone arches, Corinthian columns, blue, white, and straw furnishings—visual paradise. I don't think it's possible to think about the iconic architecture in Palm Beach without a nod to Villa Artemis. Originally built in 1916 for the Guest family by the architect F. Burrall Hoffman, this home has been in the same family for generations and was famously documented by society photographer Slim Aarons—it epitomizes the island's historically lavish chic. Last, but certainly not least, I absolutely adore the Old Bethesda by the Sea. Formerly a church that was deconsecrated in the 1920s, it's the second-oldest home on the island. Designed by Mimi Maddock McMakin, the mother and business partner of Celerie Kemble, it is a true Palm Beach original. From the pastel pink and green porch to the endless whimsical touches, every inch of it overflows with creativity. Beautiful, unique, and incredibly welcoming, it will forever be one of my favorite places to visit.

Another source of joy for me are the stunning gardens of Palm Beach, some of the most beautiful in the world. A terrific example can be seen at the remarkable Society of the Four Arts, boasting close to 170 plant species, including beautiful hibiscus, orchids, and palms. There is also an incredible sculpture garden there, complete with pergolas, as well as a fabulous offering of cultural programming. Historians, artists, filmmakers, musicians, and writers are constantly visiting for discussions, concerts, and film screenings. There is always something to see or do at the society.

And then, of course, there's Worth Avenue, the street to shop in Palm Beach. In addition to high fashion like Ralph Lauren, Chanel, or Gucci, there's Kassatly's, which sells towels and is Worth Avenue's oldest shop, established in 1923; Leta Austin Foster, a Palm Beach institution known for its luxurious D Porthault linens and children's clothing; and CJ Laing, one of the best places to stock up on cover-ups, sandals, and straw hats—items forever indicative of Palm Beach. Jessica Fontaine Swift, the co-founder of *Palm Beach Social Diary,* says, "To us, 'Palm Beach chic' means colorful cocktail attire. Think: a beautiful, flowy crepe dress paired with smart accessories. Jackets and slippers for men complete the 'Palm Beach chic' look." Another favorite shop of mine is Hive, which boasts an array of housewares and accessories and a particularly beautiful selection of notecards. And for anyone interested in monogramming and embroidery, Lori Jayne Monogramming is a treasure.

Following pages: One of Palm Beach's many marinas.

> # 66 Soft, warm climate, and the social side of the life; a life lived lazily on the broad hotel verandas, on the beach, and among the palms. 99

Vogue, 1903

Tucked away just off of Worth Avenue, there's Via Mizner—a dreamlike courtyard on the National Register of Historic Places that has lovely restaurants where you can dine al fresco. Two of my favorite Palm Beach restaurants, Renatos and Pizza al Fresco, are also in this via. Worth Avenue continues to shine even after the shops are closed for the day; at night the palm trees are lit from below, and the effect is magical. I often think of Grace Coddington's advice: "Always keep your eyes open. Keep watching. Because whatever you see can inspire you." Nowhere in the world is that truer for me than in Palm Beach. I always encourage people to look up on Worth Avenue and take in the stunningly beautiful gardens hanging above them. However, a trip to Worth Avenue does some serious double duty, as it is also one of the absolute best places to people watch.

Just as I did as a little girl, I still cherish the simple pleasures of Palm Beach— the sun, the ocean, fresh pineapple juice, and Sprinkles, which might just be the best ice cream cone I've ever had. I still always order the same thing to this day: fresh coconut with rainbow sprinkles—tried and true perfection. Another place I love to visit is Green's Pharmacy. An institution since 1938, it has a traditional

Aerin Lauder preparing the outdoor dining table at her home in Palm Beach. *Previous pages (left):* A Lilly Pulitzer dress, an iconic staple of Palm Beach. *(right)* Nothing says prep style better than this classic whale pattern. *Following pages:* Palm Beach's Worth Avenue is known for the amazing shopping.

soda fountain counter where you can get the best grilled cheese sandwiches and vanilla milkshakes in town. "An old-school drugstore with the best ice cream sodas and malts on the island. Everyone goes there after a day in the sun," Michael Kors said about Green's. You'll also find things like Whitman's Sampler boxes of chocolates and classic water toys. Walking into Green's is like stepping back in time; the entire place is pure nostalgia. The vibrancy and allure of Palm Beach doesn't dull at night; in fact, it may even get more colorful. The island has a long history of having a wonderful social scene, and evenings spent there are like nowhere else I've been. I adore having dinners at home with friends or family, but I must admit it's a really special place to go out at night as well.

With their love of Palm Beach, my grandparents were iconic fixtures on the social scene of their day. Someone once told me that when Estée threw a dinner party in Palm Beach, being asked to attend was like receiving an invitation to Buckingham Palace, and I've always loved that comparison. She invariably had a party on the long weekend of Washington's birthday, and many people would plan a trip to Palm Beach that weekend to be sure not to miss it. The guest list was a who's who: the Duke and Duchess of Windsor, the Begum Aga Khan, Sir Douglas and Lady Fairbanks, Mr. and Mrs. Frank Sinatra, Mr. and Mrs. Alexander Liberman, Mrs. Nicholas duPont, Mr. and Mrs. Alfonso Fanjul Sr., Mr. and Mrs. Winston Guest, to name only a few. Everyone was there. There was a beautiful, expansive bright green lawn that extended from the house straight to the ocean, and after a while, even that great lawn wasn't big enough to accommodate all the guests. The menus, often written in French, consistently featured special classic dishes—Brie en croûte, caré d'agneau, gratin dauphinois. Estée loved to serve soufflé aux framboises for dessert, as well as her signature vanilla ice cream covered in champagne.

Claudia Schiffer in Palm Beach, photographed by Arthur Elgort for Condé Nast.

I still have an invitation to one of these parties that she had printed on a hot pink linen napkin—so timeless and so chic, and so very Estée.

Today, there is still a glamorous social life in Palm Beach, often infused with a touch of history. A much-loved tradition is the Coconuts New Year's Eve Gala. What has now become an island institution started many years ago (either in 1924 or 1929, the exact date remains a mystery, perhaps an intentional one), when the many Palm Beach bachelors who had been invited to dinner at people's homes throughout the year wished to reciprocate the kind gesture. Their solution was to have a yearly ball on New Year's Eve where they would be able to ask people back for dinner. It was all very formal, and the original, self-proclaimed Coconuts—Chris Dunphy, Charles Cushing, and Milton "Doc" Holden, who are named as co-founders—would all wear white dinner jackets. Very early on in its history, it became the party to go to, and it still is today. It's been called the "most Palm Beachy of the Palm Beach parties," and it really is the place to be when the clock strikes midnight. These days, the party is held at the Flagler Museum, and, ever evolving with the times, the modern Coconuts of today are no longer all bachelors repaying a social debt. With a varied membership roster that includes David Koch, Alexander Fanjul, and Bingo Gubelmann, the Coconuts are now made up of all ages and marital statuses. I've spent every New Year's Eve with the Coconuts, and I love going there and giving my uncle Leonard a kiss hello on the receiving line.

As it was for Estée, inspiration is at the heart of my love for Palm Beach. We are a very sentimental family, and our house there has so much of Estée in it—we didn't want to lose anything of hers or her amazing Palm Beach style and sensibility. Of course, I kept the blue drinking glasses she used to pour our orange juice into—I often think of them as the very first objects that introduced me to my love of all things home. I also have Estée's beautiful lamps in my bedroom. We even moved all of the objects from her Florida room and re-created it in our house. It is a beautiful space decorated with pale turquoise furniture. Estée loved that shade of blue and used it in her first packaging. The room is both one of my fondest memories and a constant reminder of how Palm Beach never ceased to inspire Estée.

Years later, the inspiration of Palm Beach lives on in me. I recently opened an AERIN store here, a location acutely influenced by the environment. In some way, every item within the store is there because it shares and imparts the love I feel for Palm Beach. Every piece is intended to show my customers how much the area means to me. Personally, Palm Beach elicits feelings of warmth and holds a connection to a deep sense of history. Sharing that with people is a great joy of my life.

Palm Beach may hold a more special place in my heart than any other place I have been. It has been nothing short of paradise for me since those days of stepping off the plane and running into the arms of Estée and my grandfather. But Palm Beach hasn't changed much over the many years I've been coming—and that's what makes it so special. Those special times in Palm Beach that I once shared with my family when I was growing up, I now enjoy with my children. Today, it is now my sons who are so excited for the trip whenever my family and I are about to visit Palm Beach. It always puts a smile on my face to see that they love it just as much as I do. And it is always my hope that whenever anyone visits Palm Beach, they sense those same feelings of warmth and history. It's full circle: My most treasured memories live in Palm Beach, and now they live on in my children, and I hope they will in their children, too.

" All Palm Beach is a memorial to the incredible imagination and energy of Henry Morrison Flagler, who knew how to give the rich what they wanted, and who knew, too, that if you were to charge enough, society will go anywhere and smilingly pay the tab. "

W. A. Powers, *Town & Country,* February 1962

Vogue

clothes to love, launder, and live in

" Palm Beach 'musts.' No socks.
Sweaters over shoulders.
Jewelry... A hairstyle known as
'the Palm Beach crash helmet.'
Luxe cars. Private jets. Yachts.
Bridge. Golf and tennis. "

Steven Stolman, *designer*

Florida

" Palm Beach feels like home. I miss the smell of night-blooming jasmine from my mother's yard, the sounds of the wild parrots at daybreak, and most importantly, the light and vibrant bougainvillea along the lake trail during an evening bike ride. "

Marina Purcell, *socialite*

" Palm Beach is home to the nation's upper crust. Both old and new money flock to this narrow island for 'the season,' and the houses that line the waterfront exhibit a vast array of design ideas and solutions for tropical living. "

Jennifer Ash, *Tropical Style: Private Palm Beach*

" Palm Beach is very special to me because it's where I brought up my children. Its strong sense of community, rich tradition, and unique style is what makes it home. "

Lourdes Fanjul, *socialite*

66 The most important thing is to enjoy yourself and have a good time. 99

C. Z. Guest, *socialite*

66 Palm Beach has always encouraged its denizens to pursue their architectural fantasies. 99

Hamish Bowles, *journalist*

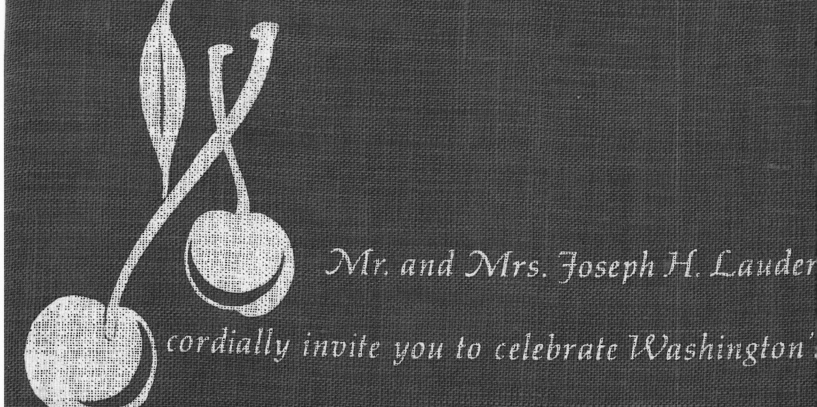

Mr. and Mrs. Joseph H. Lauder

cordially invite you to celebrate Washington'

with Cocktails and Dancing

Thursday February 22, 1968

Seven P.M. to Ten P.M.

126 South Ocean Boulevard   Pe

R.S.V.P.

rthday

Beach

"The Breakers hotel is notably a home—not a hostelry in the ordinary acceptance of the word. Year after year, the same people slip into the same suites, meet in the same corner of the rotunda, play the same games, and have the same general good time."

Palm Beach Life, January 12, 1907

"Not always sunny, but in a sunny state of mind."

Lilly Pulitzer, *designer*

"Lilly Pulitzer...Palm Beach at its best! A timeless American style!"

Diane von Furstenberg, *designer*

" We especially looked forward to leaving the gray, rainy days of London for Palm Beach at Christmas. Jack and Jackie were lent a large house on the ocean, very near Jack's family house. We were excited about being together. "

Lee Radziwill, *Happy Times*

" Palm Beach is a town of travelers, collectors, and the design indulgent. What I love the most is that I still live in the home I grew up in, which my great-grandparents built originally as a church and that my mother and stepfather have so carefully turned into a fantastical home. It has been a gathering place for generations of my family and our friends that has the magic and beauty of something built in tribute and maintained with devotion. "

Celerie Kemble, *interior designer*

" If we start things off right, it will make Palm Beach the winter capital of the world. There is no place in Europe to compare with the climate: All that is needed is to make it gay and attractive. It's up to you and me. **"**

Paris Singer to Addison Mizner

"The things that are old Palm Beach are the things that I like."

Priscilla Rattazzi Whittle, *photographer*

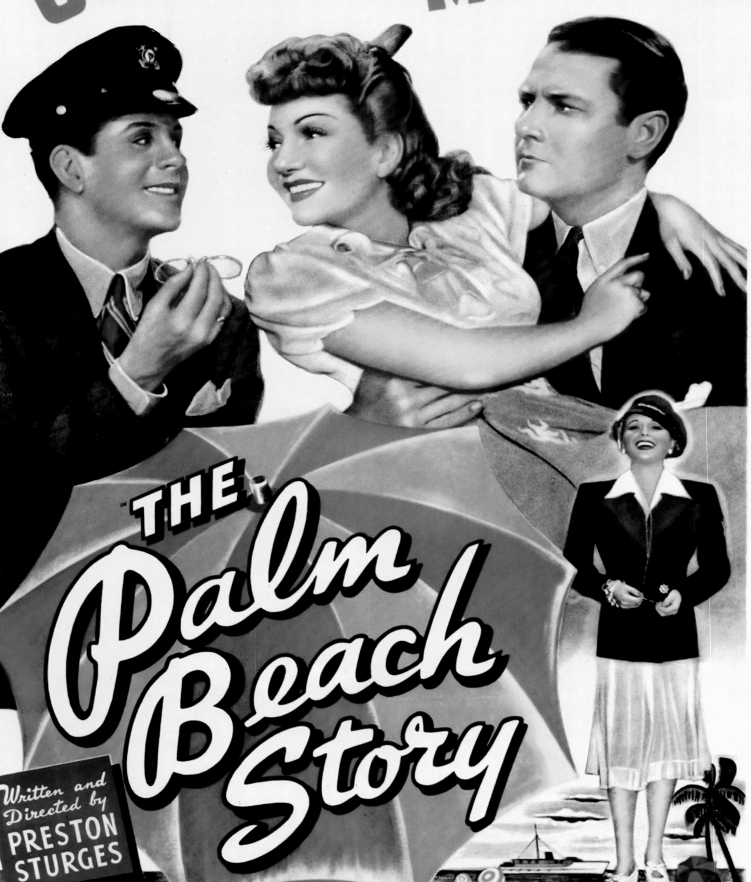

PALM BEACH BABYLON

Sins and Scandals of America's Super-rich

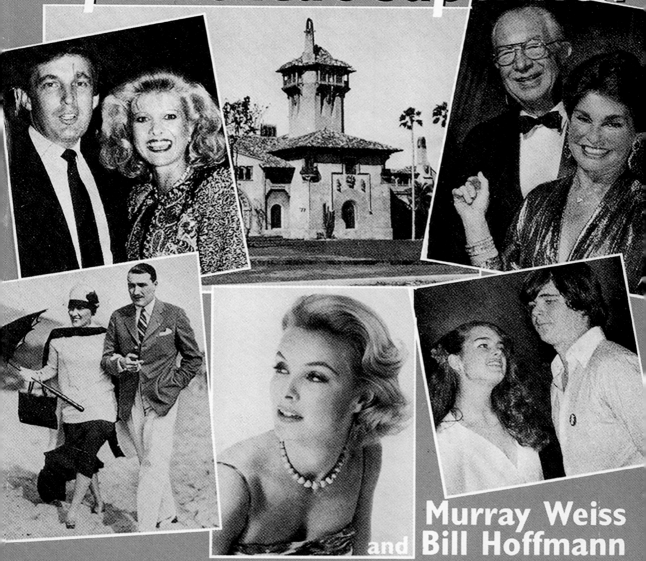

**Murray Weiss
and Bill Hoffmann**

PINNACLE/1-55817-763-9 (CANADA $5.99) U.S. $4.99

PALM BEACH, FLOR

THE SCOUT GUIDE®

PALM BEACH

FLORIDA

Vol. 5

CITY GUIDE

" Palm Beach is like a paradise, and one of the few places in America where you can not work and not feel guilty about it. There's no work ethic here. "

William J. Diamond, *town council member*

66 **Palm Beach sprawled plump and opulent between the sparkling sapphire of Lake Worth, flawed here and there by house-boats at anchor, and the great turquoise bar of the Atlantic Ocean....Upon the trellised veranda of The Breakers two hundred women stepped right, stepped left, wheeled, and slid in that then celebrated calisthenic known as the double-shuffle, while in half-time to the music two thousand bracelets clicked up and down on two hundred arms.** 99

F. Scott Fitzgerald, *All the Sad Young Men*

CAPTIONS

Mr. and Mrs. John F. Kennedy and Lee Radziwill in Palm Beach, January 6, 1963.

Outdoor dining in Palm Beach.

Left: Patron of the arts J. Patrick Lannan showing one of Bernard Kirschenbaum's walk-throughs at his art-filled estate. Photo by Horst P. Horst, *Vogue*, May 1, 1973.

Right: Jack Nicklaus and Bob Hope playing golf at The Breakers.

Artist and socialite Wendy Vanderbilt Lehman at her parents' home in Palm Beach, 1959.

A Lilly Pulitzer designer's illustration of a via in Palm Beach.

Left: Supermodel Joan Smalls in Palm Beach.

Right: The AERIN store at 33 Via Mizner in Palm Beach.

A resident biking on Worth Avenue past Via Amore.

The columned arches indicative of Palm Beach's Worth Avenue.

An old postcard of the Palm Beach Hotel.

Left: Worth Avenue and South Ocean Boulevard in West Palm Beach.

Right: Neiman Marcus on Worth Avenue.

The Worth Avenue entrance columns.

Left: Lilly Pulitzer adherents may find the designer's vision all over Palm Beach.

Right: A Lilly Pulitzer design for Prints with Purpose.

Left: LeRay Berdeau standing near the pool at Villa Today, Mr. and Mrs. LeRay Berdeau's home in Palm Beach, 1943.

Right: Alexandra Lind Rose standing on the banana leaf-carpeted hallways of The Colony hotel in Palm Beach.

Daniel Boulud serving up cocktails at his Café Boulud in Palm Beach.

Left: Interior designer Sara Gilbane in the garden of the Palm Beach home she designed for her parents.

Right: Visitors will find many colorful buildings throughout the town of Palm Beach.

Palm trees line the streets throughout the area.

The Raymond F. Kravis Center for the Performing Arts in West Palm Beach.

The fountain sculpture on the grounds of the French Regency-style Maison de l'Amitié estate, Palm Beach, 1990. The estate was demolished in 2016.

A vintage postcard featuring the Australian pine trees in Palm Beach.

Wendy Vanderbilt Lehman, grandniece of Gertrude Vanderbilt Whitney, at her home in Palm Beach, 1964.

Palm Beach's iconic The Colony hotel.

Left: The pool of The Colony hotel.

Right: Flo Smith (left) and Lilly Pulitzer at a pool party in Palm Beach, April 1961.

Poolside at The Colony hotel.

"Greetings from Palm Beach," a vintage postcard, circa 1950s.

Joan Smalls photographed by Mariano Vivanco at her home in Palm Beach.

First Lady Jacqueline Kennedy leaves a private Easter service at the Kennedy family home in Palm Beach on April 14, 1963.

Palm Beach has a young crowd, but it has been a destination for families for decades.

The Lilly Pulitzer x Barton & Gray Hinckley yacht.

Wooden powerboats tied to a dock at Lake Worth, 1930.

Left: Jean Smythe, an Ohio State skeet champion, shoots a shark with a harpoon gun in West Palm Beach, 1938.

Right: Sailing along the Lake Worth lagoon.

Princess Xenia Georgievna of Russia, Prince Andrew of Greece and Denmark, Prince Christopher of Greece and Denmark, Mrs. John McGee, and Princess Alice of Battenberg lounging in Palm Beach, 1923.

An aerial view of the grounds at The Breakers.

Left: The lobby of The Breakers, circa 1990.

Right: A New Year's ball at Flagler Mansion, January 1, 1960.

Left: C.Z. Guest and Peter Lawford, 1961.

Right: Lavinia Baker, great-granddaughter of George Fisher Baker, dancing at her Palm Beach debutante party, 1977.

Mar-a-lago, Palm Beach, 1997.

The striking colors and outdoor patio and garden designs are a trademark of the Palm Beach area.

Left: Guests relaxing on a spacious Palm Beach veranda, circa 1990s.

Right: Since 1926, guests at The Breakers have begun their visits under the distinguished arches of its porte cochère.

Society of the Four Arts in Palm Beach.

The Palm Beach Par 3 Golf Course on South Ocean Boulevard, Palm Beach.

The pool loggia of Charles and Jayne Wrightsman's Palm Beach home.

A chic Palm Beach living room designed by Lisa Perry.

Left: President John F. Kennedy playing tennis in Palm Beach.

Right: A breathtaking Palm Beach vista.

An outdoor beach area designed by Lisa Perry.

Left: A cover model for a 2005 *Town & Country Travel* issue.

Right: Model Maggie Rizer on a Palm Beach golf course.

Kelly Klein's Palm Beach home photographed for *Architectural Digest*.

Models Fabienne Terwinghe and Carré Otis leaning against a Rolls-Royce at The Breakers hotel.

Model Lillian Crawford in Palm Beach, 1970.

C. Z. Guest beside the pool of her oceanfront estate, Villa Artemis, in Palm Beach, circa 1955.

Left: Claire and Garrick Stephenson with Donald Leas, wearing Lilly Pulitzer, at Mrs. Albert Bostwick's home.

Right: A silver Rolls-Royce in the streets of Palm Beach.

The back entrance to the Mar-a-lago estate.

The garden at Broadway producer Terry Allen Kramer's Palm Beach villa.

Loggia with large arched windows at the Palm Beach home of Mr. and Mrs. Wolcott Blair.

Mr. and Mrs. Guillermo Aguilera at their Palm Beach home, 1970.

The Flagler Museum in West Palm Beach.

Left: Two things you can't escape in Palm Beach: the lush green landscape and the towering palm trees.

Right: Socialite Lucrezia Buccellati in Palm Beach.

A vintage Palm Beach postcard.

Annie Soper (riding Grey Goose) and her brother, Harrison Soper, at home in Wellington, Florida.

Front elevation of the Gulf Stream Golf Club clubhouse in Palm Beach.

Cornelius Vanderbilt Whitney, Eleanor Searle Whitney, Grace Kelly, Bud Palmer, Loriel Budge, Don Budge, Mary Phipps, and Thomas W. Phipps in Palm Beach, circa 1955.

Left: C. Z. Guest and her son in front of their Grecian temple pool on their oceanfront estate, Villa Artemis, Palm Beach.

Right: An illustration by Cecil Beaton of a home in Palm Beach for *Vogue*, February 1937.

Left: Mounts Botanical Garden, Palm Beach County's oldest and largest public garden.

Right: American industrialist Henry Clay Frick sitting in rickshaw, Palm Beach, 1916.

Three sportfishing boats—among them, the Fighting Lady of Palm Beach—head out to open water.

A napkin invitation to join Estée and Joseph Lauder at their Palm Beach home for cocktails and dancing, 1968.

Vibrant colors pop in The Breakers' Palm Courtyard.

The old Royal Poinciana Hotel Coconut Grove tea garden.

Model Fabienne Terwinghe leaning on a yellow Chrysler outside of The Breakers.

A sidewalk leading down to the coast of Palm Beach.

Lilly Pulitzer emerges from a plane clutching dress fabric, 1963.

Left: Lounging in a hammock around the Palm Beach shore.

Right: A Palm Beach home designed by Sara Gilbane for her parents.

The view from the Presidential Suite from Palm Beach's Chesterfield hotel.

Floral prints have been a mainstay in Palm Beach for decades.

The entrance of the Norton Museum of Art in West Palm Beach.

Oceanfront dining at Palm Beach's Ritz-Carlton hotel.

A dock in the Intracoastal Waterway in West Palm Beach.

Bob Leidy and Phil Brady, both in Lilly Pulitzer pants, arrive in Palm Beach to play golf, 1968.

Left: The fabled rooms of art collectors Jayne and Charles W. Wrightsman.

Right: Iris Apfel donning bright colors for her time in Palm Beach.

Kelly Klein's Palm Beach home.

The front desk of Palm Beach's Four Seasons hotel.

Left: Serving up sweets at Palm Beach's Sant Ambroeus restaurant.

Right: Vibrant colors are a Palm Beach mainstay.

The gelato stand in front of the Sant Ambroeus restaurant in Palm Beach.

The Royal Poinciana Plaza, Palm Beach.

Left: The Sant Ambroeus restaurant, Palm Beach.

Right: The bar of the Sant Ambroeus restaurant.

The Assouline boutique in Palm Beach.

Left: Assouline's Donald Robertson book in Palm Beach.

Right: Kristen Vila of West Palm Beach's Grandview Public Market, which she cofounded with husband Chris Vila.

Scenes of the Palm Beach joie de vivre.

The Lilly Pulitzer Resort 2017 presentation.

The Breakers' Florentine Fountain greets guests on the main drive.

Interior designer Celerie Kemble (of Kemble Interiors), with her three children: William "Wick" Tyson Kemble Curry, Ravenel "Rascal" Boykin Curry, and Zinnia Lacoste Kemble Curry, at their grandmother Mimi McMakin's house in Palm Beach.

The home of Katherine and William Raynor, photograph by François Halard, *Vogue*, November 2003.

John F. Kennedy and his family poolside at Joseph Kennedy's Palm Beach home, 1960.

Brothers Lee Rhoades and Grant Munder smiling atop their parents' red pickup truck in Palm Beach.

Left: The King executive suite at The Chesterfield hotel.

Right: The Presidential suite at The Chesterfield hotel.

Socialite Alice Topping in Palm Beach, 1959.

From left to right: Katie Frisbie Crowell, Sarah Wetenhall, Franny Frisbie, Kristen Vila, and Ashley B.C. Frisbie, photographed by Nick Mele at The Colony Hotel in Palm Beach.

Left: Sarah Wetenhall, CEO of The Colony Palm Beach, seated on one of the hotel's brightly colored banquettes.

Right: Chris Leidy, known for his subaquatic photography, seated at home in front of one of his photos in Palm Beach, Florida.

A vintage car parked on the streets of Palm Beach.

The exterior of the Chesterfield hotel.

Left: Sienna swings happily from the arms of her parents, Oliver "Piper" Quinn and Sara Quinn, at their home in Palm Beach.

Right: Charles and Jayne Wrightsman planted some three hundred palm trees on their property.

Left: John F. Kennedy exits his car to attend Christmas Day mass at St. Edwards Catholic Church in Palm Beach, December 1960.

Right: The exterior of Mizner Park at Plaza Real in Palm Beach.

Left: Actors Claudette Colbert and Joël McCrea on the poster for the movie *The Palm Beach Story,* 1942.

Right: The cover of *Palm Beach Babylon,* by Murray Weiss and Bill Hoffmann.

Famous and glamorous faces in old scenes of Palm Beach.

Left: Stacey Leuliette's *The Scout Guide Palm Beach* highlights the area's premier independent businesses.

Right: Author Anita Loos and the artist Cecil Beaton in Palm Beach, 1930.

Left: Known as "the Frisbie Sisters": Katie Frisbie Crowell, Franny Frisbie, and their sister-in-law, Ashley B.C. Frisbie (center).

Right: Lilly Pulitzer in her backyard, circa 1960s.

The waters of Mounts Botanical Garden.

Koi fish in Mounts Botanical Garden.

The playful hedges of Mounts Botanical Garden.

A horse comes face-to-face with a puissance wall at Palm Beach's Wellington Equestrian Center.

Rider Paige Johnson at the retirement ceremony for her horse, Beach Bum, at Palm Beach's Wellington Equestrian Center.

Left: A horse-crossing sign at Wellington's Grand Prix Village.

Right: A polo pony wearing a traditional Argentinian halter in Palm Beach.

American polo player Nic Roldan competing for team Audi in Palm Beach.

The twenty-fifth anniversary event of the Palm Beach Polo Club, March 1, 2003.

Mr. and Mrs. Harry Loy Anderson, ready for a motorbike ride, 1970.

The serene Palm Beach sunset.

Left: Mrs. Allan A. Ryan in Palm Beach, 1935.

Right: Astrid Heeren photographed by Jeanloup Sieff for *Harper's Bazaar,* 1964.

A view of the clock tower at dawn on Worth Avenue.

New Year's Eve in Palm Beach—the biggest celebration of the year.

ABOUT THE AUTHOR

A designer, tastemaker, and working mother of two, Aerin Lauder is a modern-day style icon. Committed to living life more beautifully, she founded the luxury lifestyle brand AERIN in 2012. With a love for interiors and a talent for creating warm, inviting spaces, Aerin's elegant, effortless aesthetic is a reflection of her unique upbringing. Aerin brings ease and beauty into all aspects of life and, as a dedicated philanthropist, into the lives of others.

Fireworks during SunFest, the music and art festival held annually in the first week of May in West Palm Beach. Florida.

ACKNOWLEDGMENTS

Brittany Brett; CAPEHART Photography; Carrie A. Bradburn/CAPEHART Photography; Crystal Henry/Redux; Daryl Davidoff/Davidoff Studios; Dylan Armstrong, Casey Hyken/The Dinex Group; Elena Lusenti; Elizabeth Meigher, Brooke Kelly/Quest; Escarlen Baque/TRUNK Archive; Florence Combes/ZUMA; Jerry Rabinowitz; Julia Masano/Lilly Pulitzer; Kate Powers; Kendall; Coleman/Williams Sonoma; Kyle Cowser/Shutterstock; Lavinia Baker; Lisa Olrich/National Portrait Gallery, London; Mark Lund; Marta Weinstein/The Colony Hotel; Maryrose Grossman/JFK Archives; Matthew Luttz/AP Images; Melissa Carter/Mounts Botanical Garden; Melissa LeBoeuf/Otto Archive; Melissa Sulivan/Sunfest; Miki Diosterhof; Nick Mele; Oberto Gili; Patrick Montgomery/Bert Morgan Archive; Robert Fehre; Robyn Lea; Sara Flight, Bonnie; Reuben, Shari Mantegna/The Breakers Hotel; Sara Kauss; Stephen Watt/Bob Adelman Books; Suzie Thompson/The Chesterfield Palm Beach; Tiffany Boodram/Condé Nast.

CREDITS

pp. 4, 38-39, 52, 198 (middle right and bottom left): © Lilly Pulitzer; pp. 6-7, 36-37, 68-69, 73, 122-123, 125, 134, 148, 215, 253: Slim Aarons/Getty Images; p. 8: Oberto Gili, Architectural Digest © Conde Nast; pp. 10-11, 41, 199 (bottom right): © Mark Lund; p. 14: Photo by Fred Maroon for Town & Country March 1974 © Hearst Corporation; p. 15: (top) Elizabeth Kuhner Archives, C/o Kate Kuhner Photography; (bottom) Courtesy of the Estee Lauder archives; pp. 18-19, 138, 187: © Robert Fehre; p. 20: Peter Kramer/Getty Images; p. 21: Jennifer Livingston/Trunk Archive; p. 22: Courtesy of Williams Sonoma; p. 27: Cond Nast Ltd - Arthur Elgort/Trunk Archive; pp. 30-31, 46-47, 82-83, 89, 109, 112, 130-131, 140-141, 180, 225, 229: All Rights Reserved; pp. 32-33, 110-111, 113, 114-115: © Robyn Lea; p. 34: Horst P. Horst, Vogue © Conde Nast; pp. 35, 96: Davidoff Studios; pp. 40, 79: Mariano Vivanco/Trunk Archive; pp. 42-43: Jose More/VW Pics/UIG/Getty Images; p. 45: Alys Tomlinson/Shutterstock; pp. 48, 49: Ken Howard/Alamy Stock Photo; pp. 50-51: Jose More/VW Pics/Alamy Stock Photo; p. 53: © Kate Powers; p. 54: John Rawlings/Conde Nast/Getty Images; pp. 55, 142-143, 204, 210-211, 219, 224: CAPEHART Photography; p. 56: Joel Anderson/eyevine/Redux; pp. 58, 167: © Paul Costello/OTTO; pp. 60-61: SuperStock/Getty Images; pp. 62-63: C. J. Walker/The LIFE Images Collection/Getty Images; pp. 64-65: Davidoff Studios/Getty Images; pp. 66-67: Smith Collection/Gado/Getty Images; pp. 70-71, 72, 74-75: Lesley Unruh; pp. 76-77: Found Image Holdings/Corbis/Getty Images; pp. 80-81, 231 (center): Associated Press; pp. 84-85: © Sara Kauss; pp. 86-87, 103: Clifton R. Adams/National Geographic Society/Corbis; pp. 88, 90-91: akg-images/TT News Agency SVT; pp. 92-93, 198 (top right), 202-203: The Breakers Palm Beach; p. 94: Bildarchiv Monheim GmbH/Alamy Banque D'Images; p. 95: Leonard Mccombe/The LIFE Picture Collection/Getty Images; p. 97: Courtesy of Lavinia Baker; pp. 98-99: Shutterstock; p. 101: Björn Wallander/OTTO; p. 102: Tony Arruza/Corbis/Getty Images; pp. 104-105: Allen Creative/Steve Allen/Alamy Stock Photo; pp. 106-107: John Cameron/Alamy Stock Photo; p. 116: Miki Duisterhof; pp. 117, 120-121, 61: Arthur Elgort/Conde Nast/Getty Images; pp. 118-119, 254-255: Nikolas Koenig/OTTO; p. 126, 179: Robert Phillips/Sports Illustrated/Getty Images; p. 127: akg-images/picture-alliance/dpa; pp. 128-129: Mandel Ngan/Afp/Getty Images; pp. 132-133: Samuel H. Gottscho/Condé Nast/Getty Images; pp. 136-137: Sean Pavone/Alamy Stock Photo; pp. 139, 242-243, 244, 245, 246: © Elena Lusenti; pp. 144-145: Print Collector/Getty Images; pp. 146-147: Bert Morgan Archive; p. 149: © National Portrait Gallery, London; pp. 150, 237: Photo courtesy of Mounts Botanical Garden; pp. 151, 230 (middle left, bottom), 231 (middle left), 233: Bettmann/Contributor/Getty Images; pp. 152-153: International Game Fish Association/Getty Images; pp. 154-155: Courtesy of the Estee Lauder archives; pp. 156-157: © Jerry Rabinowitz; pp. 158-159: George Rinhart/Corbis/Getty Images; pp. 162-163: Stephanie Zell/Getty Images; pp. 164-165, 235: Howell Conant/Bob Adelman Books, Inc.; p. 166: © Lisa Romerein/OTTO; pp. 168-169, 212, 213, 222-223: © Red Carnation Hotels Collection; pp. 172-173: Ian Dagnall/Alamy Stock Photo; pp. 174-175: © The Ritz Carleton, Palm Beach; pp. 176-177: Stuart Westmorland/Corbis Documentary/Getty Images; p. 181: Allstar Picture Library/Alamy Stock Photo; pp. 184-185: Erik Kunkel; p. 186, 188-189, 192, 193: © Nicole Franzen; pp. 190-191: Photographer: Ben Fink Shapiro/Royal Poinciana Plaza; p. 195, 197, 216-217, 218, 34: © Nick Mele; p. 199: (bottom left) Brantley Photography; pp. 200-201: © Charlie Wrzesniewski; pp. 206-207: François Halard/Trunk Archive; pp. 208-209: Lynn Pelham/The LIFE Picture Collection/Getty Images; p. 226: AP/Shutterstock; p. 227: Jeffrey Greenberg/UIG/Getty Images; p. 228: Movie Poster Image Art/Getty Images; p. 230: (top left) JHU Sheridan Libraries/Gado/Getty Images; (top right) Apic/Contributor/Getty Images; p. 231: (clockwise from top left corner) © The Palm Beach Post/ZUMAPRESS.com; ullstein bild/ullstein bild/Getty Images; Doug Jennings/AP/Shutterstock; pp. 238-239: Photo by Bonnie Grace Photography; pp. 240-241: Photo by Jacek Gancarz Photography; p. 247, 248-249: Brittany Brett; pp. 250-251: Alain Benainous/Gamma-Raph/Getty Images; p. 256: Toni Frissell/Contributor/Getty Images; p. 257: © Estate of Jeanloup Sieff; pp. 258-259: Walter Bibikow/Getty Images; pp. 260-261: ZUMA Press Inc/Alamy Stock Photo; p. 270: SunFest; p. 271: © Claiborne Swanson Frank Photography.

Every possible effort has been made to identify and contact all rights holders and obtain their permission for work appearing in these pages. Any errors or omissions brought to the publisher's attention will be corrected in future editions.

Assouline supports *One Tree Planted* in its commitment
to create a more sustainable world through reforestation.

Front cover design: © Assouline Publishing.
Back Cover (clockwise from top left): akg-images/picture-alliance/dpa;
Miki Duisterhof; Sean Pavone/Alamy Stock Photo; Lesley Unruh.
Endpages: © Lilly Pulitzer.

© 2019 Assouline Publishing
A Travel From Home™ Book
3 Park Avenue, 27th floor
New York, NY 10016 USA
Tel.: 212-989-6769 Fax: 212-647-0005
www.assouline.com

Printed in Italy by Grafiche Milani.
ISBN: 9781614288626
20 19 18 17